Cultural Cuisine

PAELLA

by Richard Sebra

abdobooks.com

Published by Pop!, a division of ABDO, PO Box 398166, Minneapolis, Minnesota 55439. Copyright © 2021 by POP, LLC. International copyrights reserved in all countries. No part of this book may be reproduced in any form without written permission from the publisher. Pop!™ is a trademark and logo of POP, LLC.

Printed in the United States of America, North Mankato, Minnesota.

082020
012021

THIS BOOK CONTAINS RECYCLED MATERIALS

Cover Photo: Shutterstock Images
Interior Photos: Shutterstock Images, 1, 5, 9, 25, 29; iStockphoto, 7, 10–11, 12, 14–15, 17, 19, 18, 20, 21, 22, 26, 28; Vitalli/Alamy, 13

Editor: Sophie Geister-Jones
Series Designers: Candice Keimig, Victoria Bates, and Laura Graphenteen

Library of Congress Control Number: 2019955000
Publisher's Cataloging-in-Publication Data

Names: Sebra, Richard, author.
Title: Paella / by Richard Sebra
Description: Minneapolis, Minnesota : POP!, 2021 | Series: Cultural cuisine | Includes online resources and index.
Identifiers: ISBN 9781532167775 (lib. bdg.) | ISBN 9781532168871 (ebook)
Subjects: LCSH: Spanish cooking--Juvenile literature. | Cooking with rice--Juvenile literature. | Ethnic food--Juvenile literature. | International cooking--Juvenile literature. | Food--Social aspects--Juvenile literature.
Classification: DDC 641.5946--dc23

WELCOME TO DiscoverRoo!

Pop open this book and you'll find QR codes loaded with information, so you can learn even more!

Scan this code* and others like it while you read, or visit the website below to make this book pop!

popbooksonline.com/paella

*Scanning QR codes requires a web-enabled smart device with a QR code reader app and a camera.

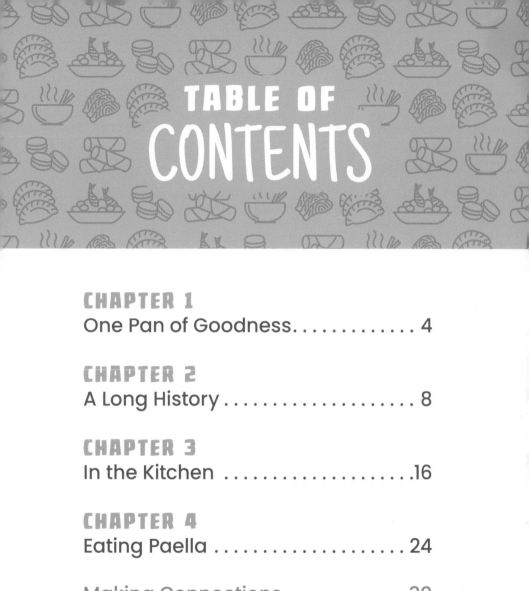

TABLE OF
CONTENTS

ONE PAN OF GOODNESS

The smell of seafood fills the air. A chef is making paella. A wide pan sits over an open fire. Rice, meat, and vegetables **simmer** inside it. Their flavors combine as the dish cooks.

WATCH A VIDEO HERE!

The name paella *comes from an old French word meaning "frying pan."*

Paella is the national dish of Spain. It comes from a part of the country called Valencia. Valencia is a city and **region** in eastern Spain. In this area, paella has been made the same way since the 1800s. Cooks combine many **ingredients** in a shallow pan.

WHERE IS VALENCIA?

Valencia is one of the oldest cities in Spain. It is located on the Mediterranean Sea. At one time, the area around this city was its own kingdom. Today, it is part of Spain.

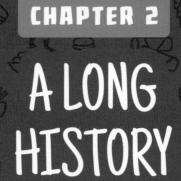

CHAPTER 2

A LONG HISTORY

Paella is a rice dish. But rice did not always grow in Spain. More than 1,000 years ago, Arabic travelers brought the crop to Spain. Rice has been a part of Spanish dishes ever since.

LEARN MORE HERE!

Rice grows in fields that are flooded.

People from Valencia often cooked

big dishes of rice with meat and

vegetables for celebrations. Cooks often

Traditional paella is made with tavella beans, which are rare outside of Spain.

made this food outdoors. They mixed

everything together in one wide pan.

They placed this pan over a fire.

In 1840, people started calling one of the rice dishes Valencian paella. The dish contained rice, beans, spices, and meat. At first, chicken and snails were common

Cooks often use a long, flat spoon to mix the ingredients together.

Today, some people use grills to make paella.

meat choices. But the dish changed

as more meats became available.

People began using rabbit or duck too.

Some versions of paella include squid ink. The ink gives the rice a dark color.

Over time, paella spread to the rest of the world. As it moved, people made their own versions. Today, seafood paella is a popular option. This version uses fish or **shellfish**. Some paella cooks add squid.

CHAPTER 3

IN THE KITCHEN

A cook uses one pan to make paella.

The cook begins frying the meat first.

Next, the cook adds the beans and

artichokes. These vegetables cook with

the meat. Their flavors blend together.

TRY A RECIPE HERE!

The meat is cooked first because it requires the highest heat.

SAFFRON THREADS

Saffron is one of the world's rarest spices. It comes from a purple flower called the saffron crocus. Each flower only has three threads of saffron. The strands are red. They have a **distinct** flavor. It takes 1,000 flowers to make 1 ounce (30 ml) of the spice. As a result, saffron is very expensive. But a tiny amount can season a whole dish.

The cook pours in chicken **stock** next. Then, the cook adds the saffron. This spice adds a

Rice is traditionally added to the paella pan in a cross shape.

distinct flavor. It also gives the dish its famous yellow color.

Later, the cook adds the rice. Paella uses **short grain** rice. This rice absorbs a lot of liquid. The paella is then left to **simmer** for 20 to 30 minutes.

People start scooping paella from the edge of the pan. That way, each diner gets part of the crust.

Cooks do not stir paella while it

cooks. Once the liquid is gone, the paella

is ready. Good paella has a slight crust

on the bottom. This tasty crust is called

socarrat. It absorbs all the flavors as the

ingredients cook.

RECIPE CHECKLIST

PAELLA INGREDIENTS

- ◇ 1 pinch saffron
- ◇ 1 pound chicken cut into 2-inch pieces
- ◇ 1 pound rabbit meat cut into 2-inch pieces
- ◇ 2 teaspoons salt
- ◇ 4 1/2 cups chicken stock
- ◇ 3 tablespoons olive oil
- ◇ 1/2 pound green beans
- ◇ 2 grated tomatoes
- ◇ 1 clove minced garlic
- ◇ 1 teaspoon paprika
- ◇ 1/2 pound lima beans
- ◇ 1 sprig fresh rosemary
- ◇ 2 cups short grain rice

Makes 4 servings

INSTRUCTIONS

1. Toast the saffron and set it aside.

2. Season the meat with salt.

3. Add water to the chicken stock and set it aside.

4. In a paella pan, heat the olive oil over medium high heat.

5. Add the chicken and rabbit. Cook until deeply brown.

6. Lower the heat to medium. Add green beans, tomatoes, and garlic.

7. Stir in paprika and chicken stock. Add lima beans and saffron.

8. Bring to a gentle boil. Add rice and rosemary. Make sure the rice is evenly spread throughout the pan.

9. Simmer until the liquid is absorbed and the rice is cooked.

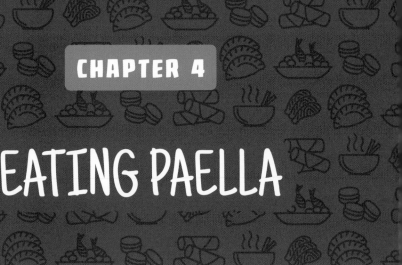

CHAPTER 4

EATING PAELLA

Traditionally, paella is eaten family style. People do not use plates. They sit around the pan and eat straight from it. Sometimes they squeeze fresh lemon juice over the top.

COMPLETE AN ACTIVITY HERE!

Seafood paella often includes mussels. Their shells pop open as the paella cooks.

Some towns have festivals where everyone eats from one huge paella pan.

People often cook paella for big gatherings. They usually eat paella for lunch. In Spain, lunch is the biggest meal of the day. People often eat lunch in the late afternoon. Dinner is eaten much later in the evening.

DID YOU KNOW?

A world-record paella was cooked up in 1987. The paella weighed 11,000 pounds (4,990 kg). It served 30,000 people.

Traditional paella is still cooked over a wood fire.

Restaurants all over the world serve paella. Some make Valencian paella with the traditional **ingredients**. Others cook seafood paella. Still others invent their own versions. They add different spices and ingredients. However, to people from Valencia, only the original recipe is true paella.

MAKING CONNECTIONS

TEXT-TO-SELF

Would you want to travel to Valencia and eat paella? Why or why not?

TEXT-TO-TEXT

Have you read books about the history of other foods? What parts of the world do those foods come from?

TEXT-TO-WORLD

People in Spain often cook paella for big gatherings. What food would you make if you were going to serve lots of people?

distinct — unmistakable and unique.

ingredient — one substance used in a mixture.

region — a broad geographic area with similar features.

shellfish — a creature that lives underwater and has a shell.

short grain — rice that is shorter in length than other rice.

simmer — to boil very gently at a low temperature.

stock — a flavorful liquid made by boiling meat.

INDEX

ONLINE RESOURCES

popbooksonline.com

Scan this code* and others like it while you read, or visit the website below to make this book pop!

popbooksonline.com/paella

*Scanning QR codes requires a web-enabled smart device with a QR code reader app and a camera.